Selected Poems

Alaska &
Northwest

Alaska, Alberta, British Columbia, Washington

Yeldagalga Publications LLC, Haines Alaska

Also by Richard Lee Harris

Reimagine: Poems 1993 – 2009

Read his poetry blog at www.blog.richardleeharris.net

Selected Poems

Alaska & Northwest
Alaska, Alberta, British Columbia, Washington

Richard Lee "Dick" Harris

Selected Poems: Alaska & Northwest
Alaska, Alberta, British Columbia, Washington

© 2013, text by Richard Lee Hariis

© 2001, cover art by Helen Harris

All photographs by Richard Lee Harris.

Back cover photgraph by Mark A. Zeiger

All rights reserved. No part of this book may be used or reproduced by any means, graphic, electronic, or mechanical, including photocopying, recording, taping, or by any information storage retrieval system without the written permission of the publisher, except in the case of brief quotations embodied in critical articles and reviews.

Published 2013 by Yeldagalga Publications LLC
PO Box 1316
Haines, AK 99827-1316

(907) 314-0242

www.Yeldagalga.com

ISBN: 978-1612240046

Printed in the United States of America

Cover and interior design by Richard Lee Harris and Mark A. Zeiger

Artwork by Helen Harris, "Top of the World," 2001

First Edition

This title is also available in e-book versions for Kindle and other electronic readers.

Find out more about the author at www.richardleeharris.net.

To those who seek beauty in the ordinary.

Table of Contents

Foreword   1

Preface   3

Alaska

Spring & Summer
- "A thousand miles north…"   7
- Eye of the Raven   8
- Sunday Morning on Berners Bay   9
- Distant Messages   10
- Arctic White   11
- Fields of Enchantment   13
- Sarah Alexandra   15

September–October
- "End-of-the-Trail"   19
- An Alaskan Autumn Passes   20
- Forest Path   21
- Anthem for *The-People*   22
- *Winnowing Wind*   23
- Will We Dance and Be Free?   25

Western Canada

Alberta
- Dancing Place   29
- The Commute   30
- Sanctuary on the Saskatchewan   31

Cousins' Last Reunion	32
Advent to Spring	33

British Columbia

Where the Silent River Bends	37
Boreal Matriarch	38
Jasper National Park	39

Washington State

Spring

"Born in ice melts and trickling creeks…"	43
Over West Bakerview Bridge	44
Wetland Spring	45
Great Blue Heron	46
The Ferryman	47
Ducking Spray	48
Never Been in a Canoe	49
Backwater Pool	50
How This Eagle Came To Be	52
Horn of the Ram	54
Devil's Club Walking Stick	55
Lesson in Bigotry	56
Last Fielder	57
Early Dusk	58
Memorial Day	59

Summer

At the Lake	63
Serenity	64
Farm Team	65
Paint Roses For Me Today	67

Summer Shower	69
Candescence	70
Words in Silence Speak	71
There Breaks an August Day	73

Autumn

Chrysanthemum Days	77
The Dreary Season	78
Seized by Beauty	79
Voices Haunt my Valley	82
Mists of Autumn	83
Lake Crescent	86
Eight Bells Toll	87

Winter

Signs of Winter	91
Old Rose	92
Eagle Feathers and Rainbow	94
From Rockport Bridge	95
Chak-Chak, the Skagit Bald Eagle	96
Winter Chores During World War II	97
"In the season of advent, in the days of long nights…"	98

So To Speak…

Truth in Silence	101
Academician	102
Vociferant Pillars	103
Shadows	104

Author's Note   105

Foreword

In *Selected Poems: Alaska & Northwest*, Richard Lee "Dick" Harris' most recent collection, remains, to my thinking, a poet of place; his words, elemental and concise, range from poignant haiku to melancholy lyric. Having myself lived, read, and written for years in the Pacific Northwest, I find in this work a sensibility not out of line with the writings of Richard Hugo, Theodore Roethke, and William Stafford; poets who, I'd like to believe, would acknowledge the sensitive nature of these words, as well as the beauty that they hold. This is a work well worth reading; and having read it, I'd recommend you gather your breath, look about your room, and settle in to read it once again.

—W.S. Merk, poet, Juneau, Alaska

2

Preface

When our children were in their teens and my wife and I began traveling further than the grocery store, we told each other that we'll travel now, noting our experiences, no matter how ordinary they may seem at the moment, because someday when we aren't able, we'll have these memories. *Alaska & Northwest* is a selection of the more significant and unique experiences in Alaska, Alberta, British Columbia and Washington State, transcribed as poems.

We frequently combined family visits with pleasure, taking advantage of as many sights as our resources allowed. Some of the poems in this collection travel back into my teen years during World War Two in the North Cascades Mountains of Washington State.

For ease of reading, backstories and clarification notes are with the appropriate poem rather than as notes in the back of the book. These poems have primarily circulated among local readers. Now, I want to share these ordinary, yet unique experiences with you.

Some of these selections have previously appeared in:

Gillilam, Mary Elizabeth and Norman L. Green, eds, *Clover: A Literary Rag*, Bellingham, WA: The Independent Writers Studio, Summer, 1012.

The Journal of the Whatcom County Historical Society, Bellingham, WA: December 2012.

Oberon Poetry Magazine. St. James, NY: Oberon Foundation, 2002.

Park Place Post (newsletter). Bellingham, WA: Cordata Park Place, October 2011.

Scroll: A Little Magazine, Bellingham, WA: SunPorch Productions, Spring, 1996.

The Storytellers. Bellingham, WA: SunPorch Productions, 1994.

Tough Guys Don't Give Up. Bellingham, WA: SunPorch Productions, 1996.

Time Pieces (Millennium Edition of Whatcom Writes!, Bellingham, WA: SunPorch Productions, Summer/Fall 1997.

_____, 1999.

Whatcom Writes!, Holiday/Year's End 1998 issue, Bellingham, WA: SunPorch Productions.

Whatcom Writers & Publishers (newsletter), Bellingham, WA, September 2010.

_____, May 2012.

_____, July 2012.

_____, November 2012.

_____, March 2013.

Alaska Spring & Summer

"Morning on the Chilkat" Haines, Alaska 2012.

A thousand miles north, I walk along River Road and tidelands as the Chilkat melds into Lynn Canal and afternoon shadows of the Chilkat Range. I stroll past dandelions in multiple bouquets and remnants of snow in an off-ditch decorated with swamp lanterns, a winter coat over my shoulder.

Lunch is trout freshly caught and beach greens newly picked. Dessert is spring's first rhubarb.

Politics are with a crew filling chuckholes and replacing collapsed sewers at the Main Street intersection where the thermometer reads 57 degrees. God is with the pantheist totem between Mountain Market and the town library celebrating "where they go to learn by themselves."

Only the eagle sees beyond glaciers.

Haines, Alaska

Eye of the Raven

And the Raven, never flitting
Still is sitting, still is sitting…
　　　　—Edgar Allan Poe

You,
in your black and satiny cloak,
unruffled and preened.
So proudly perched on cables
connecting my house and the world.

Solitarily sitting, minutes at a time,
a mass of cognitive neurons,
synapses unencumbered
with worrisome abstractions,
eyeing every move.

Icon of folklore and legend,
with criminal and capricious spirit,
how do you adapt and recall
images so keenly observed?

　　　　　　Haines, Alaska

Sunday Morning on Berners Bay

Sunlight shows on Chilkat Peaks, clouds shade Lions Head,
the tide is out, wind calm, the bay's placidity
broken by an outboard's wake lapping the shore.

Anchors, chains and rusted skiffs enfold in sand,
fishing boats are tethered at high tide,
marshmallows lay, gritty, in cold ashes.

Lupine buds, buttercups, and wild iris leaves,
wilt in a Dixie cup; funny face squiggles etched
in the sand by bicycle tires and walkers' heels.

A crow, Styrofoam shards in its beak
settles beside a sandy drive. Two more
glide out of trees behind the lodge

rob a duck pumping his wings to skim the
water's edge. An eagle circles, alights amid
squawking seagulls feeding on tidal leftovers.

A preacher sits near a wooden cross, writing
her sermon; two walkers approach, nod and pass.

Lynn Canal, Alaska

Distant Messages

Kayaks surf these frigid waters,
ferries wash glacial boulders,
windmills electrify the breeze,
red-winged flies buzz.
Northern tits dart and chirp amid rocks.
Distant messages, rhythmic waves, echo.

Lynn Canal, Alaska

Arctic White

Fog lifts
hangs
a black curtain
over cobalt leads
ever-widening breaks
in the melting floe

Tundra falls into Beaufort Sea
snow dissolves
translucent in ascendant sun
eggshell
amber
iridescent pearl
glacial blue

Wind sculpts the arctic ice
with shrill dissonance
of an Iñupiaq song

White on white
lemmings dart
escape fox

Whalebones
scattered and bleached
shadow footprints of sow and cub
coated with whitish streaks
over urine-soaked down

A storm churns
off Brooks Range
swirls
crashes
pushes statuary asunder
chaos
fractured relics
    Point Barrow, Alaska

Fields of Enchantment

A traveler asks:
  "When did Gustavus begin?"
The elder answers:
  "One night, Creator closed his eyes
  in fitful sleep;
  With a willow whip from the river bank,
  He scratched the alluvial sand;
  And that is when Gustavus began."

Our catamaran slips out of Auke Bay and glides across Lynn Canal into Saginaw Channel. We cruise around Admiralty Island and into Icy Strait between Chichagof Island and the Chilkat Range, past Point Adolphus and Pleasant Island, to the long, long pier that crosses mud flats to the beach and gravel lane to Gustavus, Alaska.

Life is new on this northern reach. The oldest tree is yet to celebrate two hundred years in alluvial silt laid down when the last glacier melted away. Except for water-worn wood buried in gravel and sulfurous springs rising from fermenting vegetation along Good River, this land's primeval past is too deep to emerge. That which is not submerged by silting rivers has washed out to sea.

Tlingit elders say they camped on this moraine four thousand years ago, before the blue ice advanced. They returned less than a hundred.

Vancouver passed these shores in his "white cloud," to explore and claim them for the crown. Through his spyglass, he saw little more than fans of meltwater tumbling from glacial ice. The seeds sprouting this northern garden had yet to be sown.

Across Main Street from the lumberyard, general store, and cafe that is downtown Gustavus, fireweed buzz with summertime frenzy and swish in the offshore breeze. Spruce spires and cottonwood crowns fence the horizon from the Chilkats and Glacier Bay.

> *From this conifer brake*
> *to the salty marsh's tidal flows*
> *—cowslip, iris, and goldenrod;*
> *lupine, horsetail and asters;*
> *ferns, yarrow and strawberries,*
> *native and exotic—mingle in*
> *a field of enchantment.*

Clouds balloon upward into a powder-blue sky and for a moment hang—a monument above the glaciers of John Muir.

Crows fly from their lookouts to patrol; their raucous cries disrupting my reverie.

Weekenders on all-terrain trikes jockey for parking at the mercantile porch rail, spraying gravel like buckshot in their path. They dismount and scurry through the doorway for bread and mail. Bounding out, they mount their steeds. Standing high in the saddle, and with an unmuffled roar and galloping bounce, they speed off to their chalets at Glacier Bay.

On the road that turns to Gustavus Gas Station with its computerized vintage pumps under *The Flying Red Horse*, vacationing teenagers prance and giggle.

A bald eagle appears. Soars above these fields of enchantment. It is quiet.

Gustavus, Alaska

Sarah Alexandra

An Alaskan summer day was passing,
Its twilight dancing on the water.
Evening was slipping into night,
When Sarah Alexandra was born.

River Beauties, their soft magenta clinging
To rocks where glacial ice once flowed.
Forget-me-nots were softening the dark,
When I heard her birthing cry.

Gently wrapped in great-grandmother's blanket,
And grandmother's locket gracing mother's gown,
She was baptized with the water
Of the Jordan and Mendenhall.

Namesake of generations
And natural beauty,
Moments old when I held her,
A grandfather's dream.

Juneau, Alaska

16

Alaska
September–October

"Woodland path in autumnal light" Haines, Alaska 1994.

"End-of-the-Trail"

In the month of full moon,
When snow dusts the mountains,
Bidding summer farewell.
When coho run the Chilkat
And eagles return,
We fly to *Deishu*,
To Tide-People
And the Cloud-Face Tribe.

The sun reaches down
Through filtered haze,
Marks the cottonwood gold,
Starry heather red.

Rainbow ladders, prisms of light
Climb the water,
Divide the clouds,
Dispel the mist,
Guide the People-of-the-Horizon
Over Pyramid Island
To "End-of-the-Trail."

Lynn Canal, Alaska

An Alaskan Autumn Passes

The last days of autumn dawn
cloudless and cold,
The Chilkats serrate a morning sky,
Solar rays and arctic winds paint
Dogwood and broad-leaves
burnished gold and russet red;
Sea lions bask in declining warmth;
Glaciers flow into shadowy fjords.

A single engine drones, glides the Tahkin
to Muir's calving wall,
Above migrating eagles and chum;
Skims glacial meadows, a finger's touch
From goats clambering craggy scarps.

Early shadows envelop the terrain,
October moon kindles a crystalline night.
Tomorrow begins our nocturnal season.

Haines, Alaska

Forest Path

I walk a forest path
To see tomorrow.
Woodland branches
Reach skyward,
To the Great Spirit,
God of us all.

Haines, Alaska

Anthem for *The-People*

Softly she sings
Her grieving song
Of a shackled brother,
A noble spirit accused.

In ancestral tongue,
Drumming her dirge,
Of her people's song.

Her husband of many winters,
Masked by the mystical wolf,
Quietly laments
A brave brother in prison.

In Chilkat blanket,
Limp with crying gestures,
He dances his brother's song
—an anthem for *The-People*.

"Whatever else may happen,
My voice will be heard
In my Grandfather's land.

"Tell me truly,
Your innermost feelings.
Aunties: Will you pray
For your Raven?"

Haines, Alaska

Winnowing Wind

In the old world, when Minnie was young,
Grandfather spoke: *I am old. My spirit*
will soon pass from this body.
I wish to go to Akillik, one more time,
to stand on tundra sponge
where the Redstone rushes by,
pick wild berries—hunt game—
speak with spirits
in the mountains of my ancestors.
             ***

Forty miles from the Kobuk, where the Redstone is swift,
Minnie, Sara, and Elizabeth, worn and wrinkled,
stand on tundra sponge.
Youthful laughter echoes in the quiet midnight sun,
as these sisters lift their baskets to spirits in the sky.

Fifty winters have stilled this river,
fifty springs have freed the ice,
fifty summers have lapsed,
since they pulled their boats with dogs
and pushed with poles
to pick berries and hunt game at *Akillik*.

The mountain breeze fades.
Minnie, Sara, and Elizabeth whistle
for wind to winnow
chaff from berries
cascading into their baskets.
       ***

Old women! Look away!!
"Shrew bears" with long legs and vicious
snouts—beasts and spirits—lurk beneath
the trees. Signs of death! Signs of disease!
Old women! Flee!!

Kobuk, Alaska

Will We Dance and Be Free?

Yesterday, we questioned.
Today, we anguish.
People of the universe,
Our land is sinking all around.
Are we going to be?

No longer, do I dream
My innermost thoughts.
No longer, do I sing my spirit song.
Our land is sinking all around.
Will we endure?

Children-of-the-Coho,
Children-of-the-Clouds,
Children-of-the-Far-Horizon!
Our land is sinking all around.
Will we dance and be free?

Klukwan, Alaska

Western Canada
Alberta

"Saskatchewan meanders in an ancient oxbow" Drayton Valley, Alberta, Canada 1994.

Dancing Place

I dance on all the mountains
On five mountains, I have a dancing place ...
    —Gary Snyder, "This poem is for deer"

Driving Route 22
through Alberta's western hills,
a young buck,
stiff-legged and awkward,
skitters across my path,
hurdles a snow fence,
lopes into scrub
along the James,
to browse and rut.

    South of Caroline, Alberta

The Commute

During an early dawn commute
in the after-fog of a summer storm
north of Calgary
through a windshield blurred with road oil
I see tire skids in the gravel
plowing ruts to the brink of a ditch
and
a deer half-buried in turgid muck
belly up
neck twisted
one bulbous eye staring into cattails

I drive on

Calgary, Alberta

Sanctuary on the Saskatchewan

The sun hangs on the horizon,
touches wild rose fruit and frost-tinged
brush. A rippling Saskatchewan meanders
in an ancient oxbow in the valley below.

October's breeze rustles lingering
leaves on aspen and birch.
Golden tamaracks, resplendent,
radiant poplars and spruce.

Canada Geese circle an afternoon sky,
whirring insects dance their masquerade
among canes. Natural rhythms prevail
in this sanctuary from distant frenzy.

Drayton Valley, Alberta

Cousins' Last Reunion
for Gene Harris, *d.* 1994

One cold October night in an Alberta town,
    where the Saskatchewan marks
    the Rockies and the plains,
Two brothers and I sit
    at the elder's kitchen table,
    telling family stories
    until the coffee pot runs dry.

The older, operator of heavy equipment,
    his eyesight failing.
The younger had driven all day
    from his rock crusher up north.
I, a retired teacher
    on my way to the prairies
    to search my roots, and
    my father's dreams.

In the morning, we linger.

With handshakes and loving embrace, we part:
    the younger to his home;
      I, on my quest.

Our misty eyes and choked voices
    glancing away from the pain,
    afraid to break the moment,

    to leave

    what in our hearts we know
    will be our last reunion.

Drayton Valley, Alberta

Advent to Spring

Advent passes winter's longest night,
the world awaits rebirth.
A wild rose, an Alberta rose,
with burgundy stem, foliage free,
in our woodland garden rests.

When Easter dawns with life renewed,
this simple rose proclaims,
in verdant leaves and fragile bloom,
its energy and light.

Drayton Valley, Alberta

Western Canada
British Columbia

"Interior British Columbia in September" 2002.

Where the Silent River Bends

Deepening purple, white bark, and
    ochre define aspen and birch.

Crisp leaves softly echo
    the murmur of fall's demise.

Palisades reflect
    waning light and collecting mist
    in flattened brush strokes
    where the silent river bends.

    North Thompson River, British Columbia

Boreal Matriarch

She startled me
as I sped south
towards the forty-ninth parallel,
a matriarch motionless
on a ribbon of grass
between the shadowy lee of boreal curtains
emerging spring and melting winter,
and a ditch choked with cattails in murky water.

Clothed in motley camouflage—tawny,
gun-smoke and brown, tints of black on snout
and tail—she stood paramount to the multi-
wheeled menaces speeding this wind tunnel.

A solitary life, haggard from subzero survival,
calving and suckling, deceptively feigning slow
footedness and tranquility until angered by
predators stalking her offspring bedded in the
understory or startled by walkers crossing her path.

Highway 95, British Columbia

Jasper National Park

It's Sunday afternoon, tomorrow is Canada's thanksgiving holiday. We are driving through North Thompson River Valley out of Kamloops, British Columbia, on our way to Jasper National Park. We pass Blackpool, Clearwater, Red Sand, and Thunder River, metal roofs and drifting wood smoke along Yellowhead Highway.

The sun casts halos around Pukeashun, Baldy, and Sir Wilfrid Laurier, cathedral peaks in the Cariboo and Monashee Mountains. White bark and ochre foliage accented with purple shadows define aspen and birch. Crisp leaves rustle in a fall cantata.

The waitress says peanut butter on the jelly tray is for Americans. She has never been to Jasper National Park.

Blue River, British Columbia

Washington State Spring

"Upper Skagit rushes out of Canada" Hope, British Columbia 2012.

Born in ice melts and trickling creeks, the Upper Skagit rushes out of Canada through gorges, faults, breached ice age moraines and magma, it grows in voice and spirit as it flows to the Sound. Raven, salmon, eagles and The-People-of-The-River were one in word and spirit before Chechacos, King-George-People, and their books, sought to make The-River their own.

With magnanimity, The-River has borne the evils of ditches, dikes, and dams. When leaves rustle golden, it calls Wind-Spirit and Rain-Spirit to return Valley-Spirit; and when creeks quicken and fawns drop, it calls Shaman Spirit to awaken from dreaming-sleep and restore The-Valley to days before the world changed.

North Cascades Mountains, Washington

Note: Skagit is pronounced *'Ska-jĕt.*

Over West Bakerview Bridge

Time-and-temperature reads forty-one,
a wind-chill takes refuge in my bones,
as one step pushes another
over West Bakerview Bridge.

Shopping mall drainage and holding pond seepage
flow through a culvert beneath,
and pass two fir saplings into a mature stand.

White bells dot spring-green Indian Plum bushes.
Swamp willow stems hold catkins erect.
Skunk lanterns radiate a cool yellow.

Mangy rabbits sniff, hop
between paper cups and plastic bags.
Stellar Jays flit from perch to perch,
squawking their displeasure.

It is the first day of spring,
my head is elsewhere.

Bellingham, Washington

Wetland Spring

Our wetland spring is
emerging from its cocoon.
The pink and white path
is a carpet of petals
where a robin is singing.

Bellingham, Washington

Great Blue Heron

... slowly the fishing holy stalking heron
   —Dylan Thomas, *"Over Sir Frank's Hill"*

Elegant
Blue-gray
Impassive
Standing
Tall as a child
In an undulating wetland swale
Awaiting imperceptible winces
Of toads and hatching larvae.

Bellingham, Washington

The Ferryman

Stout and strong, a man of few words,
he waves a log truck on, holds another back.
He knows when the ferry is loaded for a
river running high, a river running low.

Hand-over-hand, he turns windlass handles,
winches cable, shortens tackle shackled
to the line sweeping up to a carriage riding
the skyline between spar-trees on either shore.

He anchors the windlass wheel, hurries
to the bankside apron arm, climbs onto
its counterbalance, grabs the top rail,
pushing his weight downward, leveraging
its fulcrum, lifting the apron. He kicks
a bail over the end, secures it to the deck,
scans the current for swirling debris.

Perched at the stern, he drives his pike into
the gravelly shallows, pushing it from the calm
of a log boom lea into the ricocheting current,
towards the other shore. Overhead,

the carriage rattles, jerking with each
roll of the current. The skyline vibrates,
sings as its spar-tree guys shimmy and strain.

He unchains the windlass anchor,
stomps on a brake pedal,
slowly unspooling cable widening
the ferry's angle, reducing its speed.

Upper Skagit River, Washington

Ducking Spray

River rising, ferry shutting down. Slough over road. Send kids to landing. Meet bus other side, Fred take them on power line road. The school director sent the note up the hill from his station in the post office in brother's store to the big kids' teacher. She tells her sister-in-law, our teacher.

They lived together; they like excuses to close school. I like excuses, too.

I shove my books into my desk. Jump up. Bang seat hinge. Push other kids away. They push back.

I run, skipping, downhill, stomping puddles, splashing girls. Sing in my head, *I get to ride the ferry without Mom nagging, without Dad getting mad, as it plows the river. Ducking spray, high stepping rollers washing over the deck, that's real fun!*

"Stop!" my sister orders, "Mom said if we can't ride the bus on the ferry, we go to Frankie's house."

Rockport, Washington

Never Been in a Canoe

"Get in!"
Marcus hollers over a deafening river.
"We're goin' wid'out chuh."
"Hurry up, *chicken shit,*" Frank yells!

Marcus, fourteen, staggers
to keep his footing in the canoe bow,
leans on the pole he thrust into shallows
until it bends, holding the canoe in place.

Frank, thirteen, in the stern,
teeters in a wobbly balance,
pushes his pole downward
to steady the cedar shell.

I wade into water slapping
my knees. Grab the gunnel.
I'm almost nine, never been in a canoe.
"'Not *chicken shit,*" I whimper.

I glance at the river—
an uprooted cottonwood is diving,
rolling in the current,
coming right at us.

I look down. Shiver.
Blurt,
"It's not yours! You
dragged it out of the brush."

"Damn it, *chicken shit.*
Get in!"

Upper Skagit River, Washington

Backwater Pool

I wandered along a cow path meandering over an old riverbed, past woodland strawberries, through a cottonwood stand, into a sweetgrass meadow where our cows grazed and Indian-plum bushes hid robin eggs, to a backwater pool at the edge of a Sauk River slough. Until I was twelve and the war was over, and Dad bought a ranch up the road, it was my place to be alone, my place to dream. I would lie in the damp grass beside that pool crowned by treetops brushing the sky, and gaze into my reflection, with its illusive depth caused by tadpoles swimming from shallow to shallow, broken by scattered dimples of skittering striders; briefly darkened by an occasional cloud.

I drove down the new county road a few yards, fifty years after leaving the backwater pool. A culvert diverts the slough. Blackberry tangles obliterate the cow path in a riverbed of cheatgrass and wild clover. The cottonwoods are gone, logs stacked at tidewater. The meadow was a jungle of alder and swamp willow: the pool, a quagmire of skunk cabbage and devil's club. Robins, water striders and toads are nowhere. Barking dogs guard nearby rentals.

Last night, during those restless hours when dreams are most vivid, I wandered along that meandering path through the old riverbed and into the sweetgrass meadow. I knelt in the damp earth to gently turn leaves sparkling with diamond-studded droplets from last night's dew and tasted the gritty sweetness of wild strawberries. Clusters of early-season fruit festooned the Indian-plum bushes hiding robin eggs. I lay beside the backwater pool and gazed at my reflection beneath a canopy of maple and cottonwood foliage as water striders skittered and transforming tadpoles swam in the shallows. No sounds disturbed nor shadows darkened.

Upper Skagit River Valley, Washington

How This Eagle Came To Be
for Marge Martin Emmons, Upper Skagit Tribe
July 21, 1914-April 22, 1995.

A long time ago—
The Skagit splashed on rocks where wild goats fed,
Eagles rested in cottonwoods by quiet waters.
All beings spoke one tongue.
First-People and animals lived in harmony.

One day, Creator came to this place—
Sun was smiling. Clouds were sleeping.
Wind was touching twinflowers, tasting berries.
An eaglet danced in her virgin feathers.

Creator sang—
This eagle will soar over clouds,
Sing a caring song for all people,
Follow prophets to far mountains and rivers.
Gentle and wise, mindful of righteous paths,
She will see beyond horizons and tiny stones.
My spirit will be in her.

Then Creator said—
In the days when darkness leaves this valley,
When rain dances on the snow
And forget-me-nots are kissed by the dew,
This eagle will fly to her cedar tree,
To a totem crowned for eternity.
Her spirit will be forever free.

North Cascades Mountains, Washington

Note: I first read this poem on April 28, 1996, during a memorial ceremony presenting an eagle carved in cedar to the North Cascades National Park in memory of my mother's friend, Marge Emmons. This dedication was in the North Cascades Interpretive Center, Newhalem, Washington, a few hundred yards from her birthplace on the Skagit River. A lifelong nurse, she was born in July when twinflowers bloom. She died in April when winter's darkness was leaving the valley.

Horn of the Ram

A constellation flickers in half-life measure
a millennia from my eyes.
Spiraling horns in logarithmic splendor
expresses its rage in the night skies
with lightning and thunder.

Bellingham, Washington

Devil's Club Walking Stick

An elder speaks in solemn tones:
In spring when leaves are full
and bark slips away,
select a stalk of devil's club.

Cut it to fit your grip.
    Carefully peel the devil's thorns.
    For a season, cure the naked staff.
    Use a shoulder blade of a deer,
    to bone it smooth and dense.
    Wrap your handhold with rawhide,
    string your amulet of beads and hips.

    Quietly, take your walking stick
    through shadowy thickets to the river.
    Listen for an inner spirit speaking.
    You will feel your walking stick's magic
    as those evil spirits sneak away.

                South side of the Skagit River
                 Rockport, Washington

Lesson in Bigotry

Come on, Harris.
We'll beat the bus!

How?

Take the canoe hiding
in the brush by the river.

River's too high—
we'll drown!

'can't drown.
Canoes don't tip.

***

Grab 'hold--drag!

Can't.
It don't belong to us.
'belongs to Frank.
He'll see us.

'borrowed it last summer.

You stole it!
'not going,
'might wreck it.

He's *Siwash*,
he don't care.

Upper Skagit River, Washington

Note: *Siwash* is an insulting term in Chinook Jargon for a native person. It is possibly a jumbled pronunciation of *sauvage*, the voyageurs' French term for any member of an aboriginal people, the equivalent to savage or wildman.

Last Fielder

The bell rings, and
we have to go to English class.
Our teacher is big,
big as a Sherman tank,
an Amazon woman.

When she tells me to go
to the blackboard and
diagram a stupid sentence,
I don't say no. I go.

A town kid taped
a tack to her chair.
She sat on it. Didn't flinch!

Gerunds, adverbs: do they
diagram up or down?
Do they go with nouns, verbs?
Nobody cares. I don't.
I'm going to be a logger,
drive truck, a bulldozer,
go to movies, drink beer.

I'm not going to be last fielder,
and never get to bat
during noontime recess.

Concrete, Washington

Early Dusk

Swallows dart in early dusk,
glide in the stillness.
A duck spreads his landing wings.
Robins trill their mates.
Someone wakes me from my dream.

Bellingham, Washington

Note: A *tanka* for Saigyô (1118-1190), traditional Japanese nature poet.

Memorial Day

for Mark Harris, 1893-1918

A cloudless sky,
   a day filled with spring,
   a day to remember those
   who lay in common ground,
Fallen without honor,
   unseen by us,
   whose flags they bore.

As volleys resound in sharp salute
   and banners dip to a trumpet's call,
it is our day to remember
   the plaques that cling to crumbling walls,
   and plead as we pass by:

Tell them of us and say,
for your tomorrow,
we gave our today.

                    Bellingham, Washington

Washington State Summer

"Serenity Harbor" Roche Harbor, San Juan Islands, Washington 1994.

At the Lake

Clouds tinted gray, pink, and yellow,
ceil the firmament, ominous
recesses hold rain. Southwest breeze
ruffles the water. A brace of
geese honk at the dock, talking about
yesterday, today, tomorrow.
A lone eagle drafts above bass
listening in the reeds. Swallows
comb and dart beneath blue fractures
camouflaging a new insect hatch.

Lake Nahwatzel near Shelton, Washington

Serenity

An afternoon breeze rustles madrone and maple,
tosses shoreline blooms and ripples the tide.
A deer stands in speckled foliage.
Drifting clouds mask the sun
as evening calms the sea.
Daytime sounds hush.
Time is measured.

Roche Harbor, Washington

Farm Team

A second grader, too small to be asked to play, I sat on the back steps of our two-room Rockport School watching the big kids in a game of "workup." A foul ball fell into my lap.

When World War II ended and seventh graders rode the bus down the valley to a consolidated school, I was mistakenly called to the mound to pitch against the eighth grade. Although these events were years apart, they were tied together in my imagination and told me that I was to be a major league pitcher.

I was convinced that if I followed the instructions and mirrored the photographs of Bob Feller in *Open Road for Boys* and practiced diligently all summer I would be that pitcher.

I nailed some boards and a piece of tattered canvas to the fence posts at the corner of our front yard where it sloped into a dry sandy river bed and laid an old shingle that looked to be about the width of home plate a few feet from this backstop. I measured 60 feet, 6 inches, diagonally up the slope and marked the pitcher's rubber with a smaller shingle half-buried into the ground. I found a couple old baseball shells and stuffed them with rags.

Since I knew that to be Bob Feller required practice, I planned to devote Saturday mornings after chores were done and when the weather was willing to pitch one hundred strikes. This would pretty well take my whole morning, throwing the two balls through what I thought would be the strike zone, retrieving them, sometimes restuffing them, jogging out to the pitching rubber, winding up with the form described in the magazine, and throwing again.

My dad, who, from the time he entered high school, worked after school and weekends to help support his family, never played baseball. I doubt that he was ever on a baseball diamond. Needless to say, he had different plans for my Saturday mornings.

I spent them cleaning the week's accumulation of manure and bedding from the gutter in the cow barn. My pitching was not throwing homemade baseballs through imaginary strike zones. It was pitching *shit* with a five-tine manure fork through a two-foot square window behind each stanchion—scraping off the wall when I missed.

If Dad had thought of it, literalist that he was, he would have told me that I was beginning my career as every major-league player begins—on a farm team.

South side of the Skagit River
Rockport, Washington

Paint Roses For Me Today

Dip your brush, soft and fine,
In the rainbow of your palette.
With strokes sweeping and bold,
Paint roses for me today.

Paint roses that tell of heart and life,
Of spring and summer's last bloom,
Roses named for family and friend,
Roses laying upon the alter.

Paint simple roses, ancient and modern,
From distant islands and homes unknown,
Roses that decorate pharaohs' crowns,
Roses with parentage unnamed and unknown.

Paint roses high in Asia's sheer crags,
Or clutching ocean sand,
Roses hiding in woodland shade,
Roses perfuming garden and cottage door.

Paint roses that ramble and climb
In thickets we'll never transgress,
Roses showering us with bloom,
Bronze canes steadfast against the snow.

Paint roses of bards and affairs-of-state
In royal crimson and purest white,
Apricot, orange, and violet-blue,
In delicate pink escaping our eye.

Paint roses, diminutive and rampant,
Everlasting rosettes and fragile petals,
Roses fragrant and aromatic,
Wafting lemon or afternoon tea.

With your palette and your brush,
Give the rainbow its colors,
Make the sun shine, the birds sing,
Paint roses for me today.

Bellingham, Washington

Summer Shower

I lay here in the semi-light of our cabin's loft,
dreaming to the rhythm of a summer shower
raining on moss-chinked cedar shakes,
collecting in rivulets coursing the pitch,
dropping softly on June roses,
drumming elephantine rhubarb.

If it stops, Dad will call
me to the pasture
to auger holes for hand-split posts
replacing those homesteaders planted,
now rotted to the ground,
no longer defending hay meadows
with rusting, sagging barbed wire.

South side of the Skagit River
Rockport, Washington

Candescence

Midday azure fades to dusk.
Alpenglow calms the North Cascades,
paints clouds iridescent rose.
Shadows deepen icy crevasses.

The sun descends in eternal orbit
beyond the strait and Vancouver Isle.
Its flames hold back the night,
twilight dims my view.

Candescence fuels my heart
with Promethean fire.
A breeze laps the shore.

Birch Bay, Washington

Words in Silence Speak

in recognition of The Poetry Pole, *(1995 to present).*

When westerly zephyrs tease roses, and
hummingbirds hesitate their nectar search
to hear silent voices on the wind;

when the south wind moistens
earth's vagrancies in fog and mist,
these voices travel beyond;

when east wind rustles leaves,
golden tinder sparks the air,
passersby read the posted words;

when north wind blows men and treasure
to the depths of the sea,
I listen for these voices;

when the rhythms of wind and sun
are moments of peace and harmony,
slips of paper—words—silent voices,

old, new, experienced and being, are
pinned to weathered faces of a cedar stylus
with heart and spirit in an aura of love.

Yakima, Washington

Note: The Poetry Pole was planted in a rose garden by the sidewalk in residential Yakima in 1995. There it stood until last winter when Jim

Bodeen, its caretaker, moved to Selah, and planted it by the sidewalk of his new residence.

According to Jim—poet, English teacher, Viet Nam veteran, advocate for young Latinos, and founder of Blue Begonia Press—the idea of a poetry pole came to him in a vision. Encouraged by friends, he planted a four-sided cedar post "along the path of the mailman and the butterflies."

There Breaks an August Day

Between July and September,
when Sirius rises with the sun
and fog whispers to the meadow,
there breaks an August day.

Red berries hang from mountain ash,
hint of colors to come.
Rosebuds swell in final flush,
contending for summer's prize.

Cosmos in breezy display wave
above dahlias, courtly and grand.
Sea holly, suited in steely armor,
stand sentinel to a rockery.

Songbirds trill,
teach their fledglings.
Hummingbirds and bees vie
for summer's sweet nectar.

This muted day hesitates,
reluctant to pass into fall,
to vanish into winter.

Bellingham, Washington

Washington State
Autumn

"The Last Load" Cascade Days, Concrete, Washington 2009.

Chrysanthemum Days

Chrysanthemum days arrive
when trees rush to winter
and leaves lose their green
in October's first frost.

When hidden pigments are exposed,
Chrysanthemum days appear
in every hue and vibrance, in
every spectrum of red and yellow.

Walking our neighborhood
is most dramatic in mornings
when chrysanthemum days are here
and sunlight filters leaves.

It is a spectacular time
when neither eye nor pixel
captures the firestorm of color
when chrysanthemum days arrive.

Bellingham, Washington

The Dreary Season

Fog pours over the pasture from
the timberline, smothers the cows.
Out there, our horses are hidden.

Nightfall turns to rain, rattles the roof,
finds cracks in summer-dried shakes,
runs rafters, splashes as steady drips
in the coffee can by my bed.

It is the first of October,
the dreary season has begun.
With luck, it will end
the first day of May.

North Cascades Foothills, Washington

Seized by Beauty

What the imagination seizes as Beauty must be truth...
—John Keats

I stand at this precipice of other times,
seven million years in making,
new with each breath . . .

as elders tell
of raging mountains strewing
broken rocks in hunting paths;
of Warm Winds and Cold blowing
tornadoes and tidal waves;
of *The-People* fleeing great floods
washing their land;
of spurned Coyote making
coulees dry, starving *The-People* . . .

as an explorer imagines
basaltic castles and pipes . . .

as a geologist chips fossils
and hears
trembling rumbles exciting
creatures from ridge to ridge;
glaciers dissolving under transient sun
to thunder in roiling clouds
cutting valleys in millennia of orbits;
wild and boundless flora and fauna mutate
while ice dams breach Rockies

in torrents fathoms deep eroding
scablands, veering over falls,
shearing columnar matchsticks,
grinding silt fans for a hundred miles,
leaving alkaline ponds in their wake
and boulders scattered like pebbles . . .

as an artist, easel braced against the wind,
ponders this panorama for oils to
express subtleties of strata, talus,
and pools. How can he, on a flat canvas,
portray real and geologic time of
ever-changing shadows and reflections?

I remember a Sunday school lesson,
    in the beginning,
    an omnipotent being reached
    down from the firmament
    with a hand like yours and mine,
    and in Jacobean prose,
    commanded that it be.
It was!

Now I stand at the brink of this cataract,
five times Niagara's reach,
basking in October sun.

A thrush rustles the sage,
as wind gusts purge its brush;
wood ducks flutter in flight,
breaking stillness of steel-blue pools;
rodents squeak and scurry between rocks,
and rattlers stretch in a dusty crevasse.

I see truth in the beauty of this austerity,
    seven million years in making,
      new with each breath,
in the "flame-lit surface [of this] real and bodily
And living rock."

Dry Falls, Washington

Voices Haunt my Valley

And he carried me away in the spirit
         to a great and high mountain ....
     —Rev. 21.10
And I saw a new heaven and a new earth ....
     —Rev. 21.1

The days grow short, the nights cold.
The sun warms an amber haze.
Clouds play with shadows on hemlock and fir
Where frost and moisture veil the dawn.

Huckleberries turn red and russet brown,
Their fruit gleaned by bear and human hands.
Silken seeds bounce over alpine scree,
Fireweed lingers above pearly everlasting.

The river meanders its self-proclaimed course
By sandy pastures and bracken banks
Where cottonwoods quake in silver and gold
Through jams and sloughs in a westerly flow.

Voices of past labors and dreams fulfilled
Drift on a meadow breeze.
Once gone, they return
To haunt my valley.

             North Cascades Mountains, Washington

Mists of Autumn

for Rod O'Connor (1906-1995)

Clouds hang ominous and gray.
    Dusted with snow, Sauk Mountain looms
    above Skagit River to the north.

The mists of autumn shroud the valley.

Steadied by his cane and my brother's arm,
    Rod lingers on a path
    through an orchard, now brush and blight,
    to what remains of his boyhood home.

With voice trembling and eyes tearing,
    days before his 89th birthday,
    he recalls the past.
    The years collapse.
    ***

My family is Irish-Catholic.
About 1900, they with my aunts and uncles and cousins
settled on this side of the river between here and the Cascade.

I was born on Stafford's deserted ranch
    one cold January day in nineteen-oh-six
    on the south bank east of Barnaby Slough.

Maggie Barrett,
midwife to just about every newborn in the upper valley,
poled her dugout from above Marblemount to birth me.

One night, before I was three years old
and we lived in the Mitchell house down by Iron Slough,
a freshet swept out of the hills and flooded our fields.

> *We all climbed a ladder into the attic to sleep*
> *after a washtub floated through the kitchen.*

Dad rowed to the barn and
> *let the stock out to higher ground.*

In spring,
> *when days lengthened and the air warmed,*
> *stubbed toes and slivers did not deny us the freedom*
> *to shed our shoes and feel the plowed dirt and cool sand.*
> *We roused the old cows and soothed our feet*
> *where they had lain.*

Harkening to a bup . . . bup . . . bup . . .
> *my brothers and sisters hustled me*
> *through salmonberries and stinging nettles*
> *to an old shack on Smith's Slough*
> *and told me that the grouse nesting there*
> *were spirits haunting the house.*

In winter moonlight,
> *we raced our shadows over frost-crusted meadows,*
> *glided across icy ponds in sheer delight.*

See these Doug firs crowding the road,
>*their girths greater than two men can reach?*
Look at that barbed wire rusting their hearts.
I was barely ten when they were saplings
transplanted as a fencerow by my father and brother Dave.
Then Dave went to war.

Before I was twelve, when school was out,
>*I walked ahead of the sled team*
hauling shingle bolts to the river.
With only gunny sacks to protect my legs,
I carried five gallons of crude oil and
greased skids all day with a dauber of vine maple and hemp.

Up the road,
>*four, maybe five, miles on the way to Uncle Harry's ranch,*
gravel-bottomed springs ran from hillside ravines
to the river and spawning salmon.
Boys no longer fish those shaded pools,
they are all fill and clear-cut now.

***

We linger with Rod in the dooryard of his youth.
> So many years lapse in these moments
as a child in his mother's arms.

Autumn shrouds the valley.

>*North Cascades foothills, Washington*

Lake Crescent

A fall breeze pushes blackened scree
into shadowy conifer duff.
Wild mint's leftover bloom, bent
under footfalls in basaltic sand,
gives autumn its perfume.

White caps roll and smother
a cold, deep-blue glacial U
created by mythic grandmother's wrath,
forever banning salmon from the sea.

Olympic Peninsula, Washington

Eight Bells Toll

A gale force blew across the sound that October night
when the MISS LINDSAY dragged her anchor
and rolled her keel
in the shallows of Portage Island
before eight bells tolled over Bellingham Bay.

Was it a rogue that broke the swell
and swamped this purse seiner,
her nets stowed and holds clean,
and drowned these fishers
of Russia's tides and Mexico's shores?

With voices hushed and tears freely flowing,
mourners still hear a crewman—
once crisp and clear—now a whisper in the wind:
Do not wait for our watch to end.
Do not wait for eight bells to toll over Bellingham Bay.

The seiner's pulsing diesels vibrate the sea
under gray and misting skies.
Its crew tosses a wreath on the quivering bay.
With their skiff, they circle
as if pursing their comrades' last cast.

They return to their stations
and sail into nightfall
leaving their tribute
to bob on the harbor eddy
in eerie afterglow of fishing lights.

Hale Passage, Puget Sound, Washington

Washington State Winter

"Signs of Winter" Rockport, Washington 1945.
Taken by 11-year old RLH with his father's 1928 KODAK box camera.

Signs of Winter

A storm sweeps from Alaska's gulf,
streaming moisture-burdened clouds
into our valley, drags fog and mist
in a counterclockwise spin; rolls over
sandbars and sloughs, scours debris.

Windfalls and eroded flotsam jam,
careen,
crash the river,
pollute its turbulence.

Gusts tear still-leaved cottonwoods,
shallow-rooted hemlocks from
saturated earth and duff-laden sponge,
dive and bob snapping their branches
with undulating arrhythmia. Roots
skeletonized as filigreed tendrils spew
frothy wake of dirt and rocks. Trailing
winds lift disgorged clouds over jagged peaks.

A chilled sky clears.

Upper Skagit River Valley, Washington

Old Rose

I see you through my kitchen window,
Wine-red canes above an ivy skirt,
Entwining a garden lattice,
In contrast to winter snow.

With spring, your foliage will cover
Our garden portal with a canopy of green.
By summer solstice, you will greet admirers
With bouquets of cerise and raspberry scent.

A century has passed since you journeyed west,
A slip in a schoolteacher's satchel,
To be rooted by her homestead cabin
In a meadow where the river once ran.

The bridal hands that nurtured you now reside
In the earth beside those who adored your bloom.
Others who lived in your cabin have gone their way
To find life's fortune where they will.

Your cabin now rests in a park,
For the curious to view.
Few remember, traveling the road nearby,
That you grew where cattle now graze.

Survivor of flood and sorrow,
How often I ponder your life,
And the generations you watched
Spring forth, prosper, and wane.
 Do you pause to recall seasons past?
Is it always the coming springs
And summers we share,

Or is it the winters of our reflection?

Old Rose, neglected and uprooted,
Origin obscure and name unknown,
Each spring you return,
A heritage rose, vibrant and new.

Transplanted from Porter Homestead
Rockport, Washington

Eagle Feathers and Rainbow

for Imogene Washington Bowen,
   Upper Skagit Tribe (1935-2007)

Looking at you now, Imogene, in your
cradle of lasting years, I see you in
our picture on the steps of Rockport School,
two rooms at the foot of your family's

sacred mountain by the river of your
tribe, so many years ago. You are
the pumpkin-faced first grader wearing
a simple wash-dress in the first row,

so sober under your freshly combed hair
and new barrette, Imogene. I'm a second-
grader behind you, all frowns and ears sticking
out, my hair slicked-down. I loved your name,

Imogene . . . Imogene. You see,
I still sing it. In minutes now, elders
will carry you away, to lower you
into an earthly bed under boughs of

cedar and snow on your sacred
mountain. As darkness hovers, Imogene,
your spirit will rise, an eagle passing
through a rainbow above the river.

Upper Skagit River Valley, Washington

Note: *Imogene* is pronounced *Īm-ŭ-'jēn*.

From Rockport Bridge

I stand on Rockport Bridge,
This sunlit winter day.
My eyes follow the Skagit
Past Washington Eddy
To Eldorado's glistening ridge.

For a fleeting moment, I see
Snowy ridges, glacial slopes,
Alpine lakes and hanging valleys,

Traces of ice from eons past.

Framed by cottonwoods and purple hills,
The road edging Mount Sauk
Scribes the river,
Gently washing pebbles
Beneath a winter sky.

Travelers pass me
In eagle search,
Skimming the view—
A ferry barge,
A cedar canoe,
Our log cabin—
Artifacts of my youth.

These incidental visitors
Will never hear eagles call,
See black bear fish,
Trout rise to the fly,
Witness stars outshining the night—
All that I see from Rockport Bridge.

Rockport, Washington

Chak-Chak,
the Skagit Bald Eagle

for Marvin L. "Jim" Harris, 1937-2009.

Perched in an old-growth forest,
Chak-Chak rouses. In morning light,
Scans the river with piercing eyes,
Searches sandy bars for dying chum.

Chak-Chak breaks silence,
Soars from Sauk Mountain,
Drifts Washington Eddy;
Glides the river's course.

Chak-Chak skims the shimmering water,
Clutches a floundering salmon,
Settles on a backwash beach,
Feeds on his catch.

Perched in barren cottonwoods,
On the south bank where the wild Skagit bends,
Chak-Chak, in stoic dignity,
Basks in warm afternoon sun.

Chak-Chak calls his mate.
Wings extended, talons interlocked
In descending flight, they tumble,
Somersaulting earthward, breaking skyward.

Before evening shadows deepen,
Purple hues of dusk chase the day.
Chak-Chak catches an ascending draft
To his nightly roost—and slips away.

Upper Skagit River, Washington

Winter Chores During WWII

Six animals in their stanchions. Mangers filled. Freshly bedded. Gutter emptied. Shit-splattered floor scraped clean.

It's a warm, moist, bovine world in this old barn. Temp will drop to ten tonight.

A pale moon, almost white, is rising over Porter Mountain, casting the barn's long shadow over its yard, down the bank, and onto the field below.

High above Sauk Mountain, Queen Cassiopeia and "Big Bear" dance around North Star.

Snow covers the ground. Been there a week. No rain. A miracle. The path through the field is packed snow. No slush. Splashing girls at school is fun, splashing in the barnyard is not.

When the Skagit is high, the meadow swales in the old Sauk River bed pond. When a northeaster blows, enough ice freezes for kids to play. Don't let Mom or Dad find out, or fall in.

Crystalline droplets glisten on straw poking through crusty snow. Ice settling on swale slopes crack. I'll follow a fencerow home. I can almost see it from here.

South side of the Skagit River,
Rockport, Washington

In the season of advent, in the days of long nights, storms sweep our valley with moisture-laden clouds streaming fog and mist blanketing sandbars and sloughs; lifting their disgorged mass over the North Cascades. Eroded windfalls and flotsam careen and crash in river turbulence. Leafless cottonwoods and shallow-rooted hemlocks tear from saturated earth and duff-laden sponge to dive and bob in undulating arrhythmia. Roots skeletonized into filigreed tendrils spew frothy wakes of dirt and rocks.

These storms happened when The-People-of-the-River spoke many tongues and The-River ran both ways. And, they will happen....

Upper Skagit River Valley, Washington

So To Speak...

"Follow the leader" Canadian Rockies, 1993.

Truth in Silence

Philosophers, politicians,
psychologists and preachers;
poets, plumbers and
physicians—sincere, erudite,
articulate—seek truth in silence.

Between or among them,
none can agree that, if
perchance, they learned
a tree has fallen in a
forest *sans tympanum*,
they will debate *ad infinitum*,
its sound in silence as it fell.

Academician

I pay my dues to a
poets' academy.

Yes, we have one, as do
proctologists and psychiatrists,

and others who wish to incorporate,
print "journals" and exempt taxes.

With directors, elected or selected,
through power self-vested,

levitate colleagues
to elevated statuses.

Admission?
Membership paid up.

Vociferant Pillars

Senators' voices
stand stelae with
static message,
lyrics that never
vary, choruses
repeated in rounds.
No matter the solo,
the weather, or
impending storm,
the words are the same.

Note: Stēlaē (pl.): a usually carved or inscribed stone slab or pillar used for commemorative purposes.

Shadows

A shadowy duo presses into a mid-summer cloudburst
and crosses my path as I drive to the 12th street bookstore.
With each swipe of the wiper,
my vision changes between detail and watery blur.

One figure—
      toothless, arthritic and clothes torn—
clutches the arm of a confident other.

I grip the wheel,
touch the brakes,
peer into the storm,
wonder about tomorrow.

Author's Note

Richard Lee "Dick" Harris grew up in log cabins without electricity, indoor plumbing, or running water, deep in the North Cascade Mountains of Washington State. As an adult he worked as a teacher, psychologist, and college administrator, mostly in Washington, while raising his three children. A lifelong writer, he turned to poetry after retiring from professional life.

Through years of adventure travel and family connections he has gained a strong sense of place from the northwestern edge of the continent—Washington, Alaska, and the Canadian provinces of British Columbia and Alberta.

He published his first book, *Reimagine: Poems, 1993-2009,* in 2010, at age 76.

Dick lives with his artist wife Helen in Bellingham, Washington.

www.ingramcontent.com/pod-product-compliance
Lightning Source LLC
Chambersburg PA
CBHW031650040426
42453CB00006B/263